Somehow Balanced

Somehow Balanced

Poems by

Ralph Stevens

© 2024 Ralph Stevens. All rights reserved.
This material may not be reproduced in any form, published,
reprinted, recorded, performed, broadcast,
rewritten, or redistributed without
the explicit permission of Ralph Stevens.
All such actions are strictly prohibited by law.

Cover design by Shay Culligan
Cover and author photos by Sally Rowan

ISBN: 978-1-63980-559-4

Kelsay Books
502 South 1040 East, A-119
American Fork, Utah 84003
Kelsaybooks.com

*For the poets who came before
and showed the way.*

Acknowledgments and Thanks

First and foremost, thanks to my readers, Andy and Jeanne Kohn, and Elizabeth Phelps, for comments that encouraged and pointed out ways to improve these poems. And to my wife Sally Rowan, for her encouragement and excellent editing, and inspiring photography. Additional thanks to Irene Toh and Alan Walowitz for their help and encouragement. Finally, some of these poems were inspired by comments by Sydney Landon Plum in her profoundly rich email list, "Today's Poem." Poems have many sources; this is one of them.

Thank you to the following publications, in which versions of these poems previously appeared:

A Bounded Space and Other Poems, by Ralph Stevens: "A Fall of Snow," "Listening in the Dark," "The Third Degree of Sorrow," "The silence this afternoon," "These Forgotten Things"
Gyroscope Review: "Hidden in This Field," "Small Sounds," "The Case with Photographs"
Red Wolf Journal: "A Bounded Space," "A Congregation of Gulls," "Beaufort Scale," "For a few months"
Sheila Na Gig: "The Craft of Loneliness," "Four and Twenty Blackbirds"
Verse Virtual, An Online Community Journal of Poetry: "A Wrinkled Wing," "Given the way things are," "Sunrise, Damariscotta"

Contents

Prologue

A poem begins   15

I: Old Sorrows

A Fall of Snow	19
The Craft of Loneliness	20
Alone with the Deer	21
The Third Degree of Sorrow	22
The silence this afternoon	23
The Work of Gentleness	24
Hidden in This Field	25
These Forgotten Things	26
Symphonic Light	28
Out into Snow	29

II: And in Which Darkness

The Museum of Beautiful Things	33
Listening in the Dark	34
The Raptor's Place	35
Heard at Midnight	36
And in Which Darkness	37
Shadow Lines	38
Given the way things are	39
The Unremembering	40
A Wrinkled Wing	41

III: Encounters

Small Sounds	45
For a few months	46
Frisbee	47
Planting Fireweed	48
The Case with Photographs	49
Like a Sower	50
Red Maserati	51
The Silver Pin	52
Holy Ground	53
The thing about tears	54

IV: A Kind of Traverse

Standing Watch	57
A Congregation of Gulls	58
The Hood	59
Am I That Crow?	60
More than Corn	61
And who's to say a storm	62
Beaufort Scale	63
When This Day Is Over	65
The Shape of Silence	66
In a Kitchen	67
Sunrise, Damariscotta	68
A Robin Stalks the Lawn	69

V: Somehow Balanced

"Take me back"	73
On the Sheepscot Road	74
A Bounded Space	76
Drink Me	77
Ex Libris	78
At Bradley's Used Books	79
Searching for Radiance	80
Four and Twenty Black Birds	81
Flying	82
Somehow Balanced	83

Envoy

Driven Rain	85

But heard, half-heard, in the stillness
Between two waves of the sea.

—T.S. Eliot

And here face down beneath the sun
And here upon earth's noonward height
To feel the always coming on
The always rising of the night . . .

—Archibald MacLeish

I am still that figure face down in the sun.

—Mark Strand

Prologue

A poem begins

somewhere—
in the channels of a
salt marsh
it might be,
with a canoe pushing
through green sword grass,
or it comes to a
clearing in the woods
as a snake
slides under a rock.
It could be anywhere—
an attic room
on a city block
where a girl
escapes to read,
while her mother
stares out the kitchen
window. Perhaps a gurney
in the ER, after triage,
or the department store
escalator, between
housewares and
women's apparel.
Poems begin, they
wander for a while,
and they end,
while wonder
lights the page.

I: Old Sorrows

A Fall of Snow

The noise of old sorrows,
old back pain and the
shouting world fade
for a moment
into a fall of snow.
The flight of wild birds
over this room last night
returns unannounced
and settles into place
alongside the books
resting on shelves.
There are even now,
they say, trees in paradise,
and dogs, and little burros,
all manner of creatures
who live quietly, who
rest in peace.
A cardinal appears,
and sits for a moment
on a branch outside,
his red
punctuating the white
fall of snow.

The Craft of Loneliness

I learned, early, the craft of loneliness.
—John Deane, *To Give Dust a Tongue*

Teachers without book or chalkboard,
they pantomime a lesson.
The man bending over mudflats,
clam rake rising and falling,
the freight that passes
unseen in the distance,
geese who do not land
but leave their raw cries
behind them over the town.
And the solitary loon,
taking off in a spray of lake water.
They are everywhere,
the teachers,
like those fishing boats
on their moorings at sunset,
even this old brown belt,
its quiet buckle scars
marking the days.
Now the heron, alone,
standing in prehistoric stillness
as the tide rises,
and brings things quick and silver,
in answer to unnamable longings—
these wise masters of solitude,
the craft of loneliness.

Alone with the Deer

Sometimes my only weapon against pain
is to go out at midnight,
not slamming the door but
walking 'til the sky wakes up,
shakes off the dark.
There are few cars on the road.
I don't lift a thumb and no one
offers the ride I would have to decline
without knowing how.
Alone with the deer
who break cover at night
to feed on tender leaves and bark,
I might have known
the fight is only with myself.
They stand in the trees
as I walk by, stare at me
not moving, wide-eyed
in recognition.

The Third Degree of Sorrow

Not the crashing wave
of sorrow in the first degree—
the child sitting in the ruins
of a bombed apartment building,
old man in the evening,
weeping on his porch,
phone ringing to announce
another cancer or miscarriage.

The third degree is
as quiet as the last light of day.
It's the yard sale
signing away the unwanted,
a child's ice cream cone,
dropped on the sidewalk,
all the castoff lost forgotten things,
dust-covered shoe, torn lamp shade
in a vacant lot, the shriveled spider
hung in the web, her work done.
Even the blue of a broken robin's egg,
far from any nest.

You were walking peacefully, but now
you wonder what happened.
And is that what troubles you,
the death, perhaps, of a baby bird?
But sorrow in the third degree
is no more than that,
a sad, soft, gentle thing,
the whisper of a small wave
as it pulls away from the beach,
and leaves the sand glistening.

The silence this afternoon

arrives with the winter light
that paints the objects in the room,
digs beneath surfaces,
colors a Boston rocker, antique dresser,
and fills the brick fireplace. Even the dust
under an end table finds texture
and the sofa cushions grow softer
with the silence.
The whole room with its
sandwich plate and apples
becomes a Vermeer still life,
and the silence falls
like shadows in a painting,
while outside the snow piles up on the lawn,
on the branches of the spruce trees
that stand along the drive,
watching the house,
without a sound.

The Work of Gentleness

It's a reminder of limits, this storm,
the lights flickering, power going out
any minute now, that wind roar
sending us to the elsewhere of memory,
haunted as by a distant train whistle.
They come back, the memories,
while we get the flashlights ready,
the kindling for the wood stove,
and sit waiting.
You were gone so long and
my voice is rough.
Now the wind picks up
and I can talk again.
We're both in the borderland
where memory lives
refreshed, purified.
Our voices grow mild,
quiet beneath the storm, telling us
we can yet succeed
at the inner work of gentleness.

Hidden in This Field

You never know what might be
hidden in this field, the one you just
walked into, where the pine woods
gave way to sunshine, the grass
brown in August heat.
There is delight
in the small blueberry patch,
the rocks, gray, humped, like
whales, and covered with lichen.
You sit down,
not because you need to
but because the field
comes to you,
your mind open to receive
what is hidden here.
Someone may have buried it,
something once held reverently,
a small thing not thrown out with
the food wrappers, Styrofoam boxes.
It may be the bird that broke
against the window thinking
it was more sky, or the kitten
stillborn in a pile of straw in the barn.
A boy found it
carried it here, buried it
in a corner of this field.
Such hidden things,
soft bird, quiet kitten and
a boy's tenderness,
appear as you now rest
on this gray rock.

These Forgotten Things

When you decide to move, this house,
the one you thought you'd die in,
disappears while you pack up the past—
old photographs, greeting cards,
your children's grade reports.
They show up, these forgotten things,
asking you to remember.
Perhaps a ruthless trashing is
what they need, boxes of mementos
bullied into piles of rubbish. But then you
stumble on the tee shirt
your daughter brought home from camp,
wrinkled now and unwashed but
fragrant too, the odor of her youth
still clinging. What can you do?
She's a woman now, and wears
different fragrances. Suddenly
it's a woodland path, this packing,
leafy and winding,
with unexpected turnings onto things
you want to keep but don't know how,
or where to put them.
It starts to rain and you
just want to stay unpacked,
here in the old house.
So you listen, say,
to the box from the
Pittsburgh crematorium, the one
that held your father's ashes.
You count ten cartridge shells
from the salute that honored him,
buried at sea twenty years ago.

The guns went silent, and what place
do they have now, the empty shells?
Is it time to mourn,
then bury this past,
the one your life has put together?
It's a mosaic in a wall,
in a room that won't be there
when you open the door
of your new house.

Symphonic Light

It's a mystery,
the thing we call paradise.
One moment it surrounds us
with symphonic light,
and disappears the next, into
the shadow of trees.
And we wonder:
is there something wrong with our eyes?
We can barely see
what we most want,
the end of all desire.
We stare into the shadows.
The forest starts to vibrate
and we hold our breath while
the grace of the world
takes possession, while
white birds circle
and the trees begin to speak.

Out into Snow

> *But the conquest of the physical world is not man's*
> *only duty. He is also enjoined to conquer*
> *the great wilderness of himself.*
> —James Baldwin, *The Creative Process*

But there are times I am enjoined, rather,
not to conquer but to leave
that wilderness of self. Which I do,
perhaps in August on a dusty
road through the pine woods,
or in winter when the heat
of the kitchen raises such a sweat
that I go out into snow.
I've had enough of that wilderness.
I look to another world, not
the one the farmers, oilmen,
the miners want to conquer.
It's the river of the great blue heron,
rocks of harbor seal, and
the hyacinth next to the house.
And the mountains. Are they not
wilderness enough without the wild
beating of this all-too-human heart?
And if I'm enjoined to conquer
that wilderness of myself,
let me find it there,
on mountain trails perhaps,
past mountain streams through
alpine forests of spruce and fir,
meadow homes of marmot, sky
of the red-tailed hawk—
somewhere beyond the door
of this overheated kitchen.

II: And in Which Darkness

The Museum of Beautiful Things

has a new exhibit,
a list of things for you to create,
to picture in your mind.
Every wall, alcove, stairwell,
is covered with labels,
items from the museum catalog.
Give it a try, see
what you can do with "Waterfall,"
"Harbor Sunset," "Alpine Pasture," "Rose Garden."
But these are easy, right?
How about "Paving Stone," "Brick Wall,"
"Windbreak," or "Cave Entrance"?
And in this other gallery
you'll find "Smoke over Tent City,"
"Broken Levee," "Burning Squad Car,"
"Cyclone on the Horizon."
The exhibit depends,
you now realize,
on more than mere fancy
but the possibilities are endless.
Don't lose heart when
you come to "Buddha
Shattered in Religious War,"
"Bombed Cathedral," "Gallows
in the Town Square."
Remember these are only words
on a museum wall,
waiting for the artist, you,
to picture them.

Listening in the Dark

> *Darkling I listen; and, for many a time*
> *I have been half in love with easeful Death . . .*
> —Keats, "Ode to a Nightingale"

I hear the spruce outside my window,
sighing in the wind. The snow last night
that frosted the bare branches
of maples along the road seems as much
reason to live as when we children
shrugged into bulky one-piece suits
impatient to grab our sleds.
The opening chords of Mozart's *Jupiter*
could fill me with the sense
that my life is complete, finished, could
make me in love with easeful death.
But why not live for at least
one more sunset over the harbor?
And there is this listening in the dark,
hearing now imagined voices,
hopeful as Hardy's thrush,
singing of something I might yet see
in the green meadows of this world.

The Raptor's Place

In a dark time the weary,
sorrowful, beleaguered by wars and
rumors of wars, thread their way
between the monstrous and the sacred.
Those lying politicians, word jocks,
are visible monstrosities,
and the path around them
is treacherous. The kestrel and osprey,
they, too, bare their claws
yet we don't blink at the daily seizing
of field mouse, herring,
to feed the shivering young.
The raptor's place is with the playful otter
in sacred territory.
We lodge with the profane
but recall that other,
sweet and balanced land,
while we content ourselves with the
local laundromat, its faint acrid smell
of soap in small boxes,
chugging washers, dryers that spin,
release from their warm cabins
clothes fresh and clean.
We get up, we weary ones,
get changed,
and head back into the dark.

Heard at Midnight

> *The Sea of Faith*
> *Was once, too, at the full, and round earth's shore*
> *Lay like the folds of a bright girdle furled.*
>   —Matthew Arnold, "Dover Beach"

The sea is calm tonight, and if
the loon that dives, porpoise that feeds
offshore, have anything to say, this
is the sea of faith although
the cathedral burned, the school bus
turned over on an icy road.
The substance of things hoped for
lies in a world in which the herring do not
think about the porpoise's huge mouth,
or fear the loon's red eye.
Yet swan and elephant will mourn
a mate's death and the dog lie weeping
on her master's grave.
The sea is calm and faith
is more than a suggestion,
even as doubt comes unlooked for,
heard at midnight,
no more than a footstep
on the stairs.

And in Which Darkness

And what there is between a man and woman.
And in which darkness it can best be proved.
              —Eavan Boland, "Quarantine"

It wasn't dark at first, not
dark enough at least.
There was too much light
in their eyes, too much
blue of sky and
the stream ran so fine.
The forest was green on gray.
There was no
smell of death.
Were they deceived by
the lack of contrast in that landscape,
all that sun and birdsong?
And later, in the house
with the children,
the roast and apple pie
on Sundays, trips
to the neighborhood pool: what
could lesson them in darkness
and why, they might have asked,
is a lesson necessary?
Do we really need the dark
to know the light, and
in what darkness
is love proved?
Give us time,
they might have said.
It will be dark
soon enough.

Shadow Lines

If it's at all worth noting
that the Venetian blinds
make shadows across the bathroom sink,
then let it be noted. The afternoon
moves the way afternoons do,
slowly, and the sun finally
reaches the right angle,
pours around the slats and
makes shadow lines.
My wife, curator of patterns,
finds her camera,
calls me to come
and have a look. There are indeed
dark bars across white porcelain.
She clicks the shutter, moves a little
to get another view. I try
to find something to say, which
I'll need for a poem.
Well, there is a shadowy texture
to life, bars across the ordinary.
Meanwhile the afternoon sun
does what it always does,
makes some lines, then
drops lower and the sink
goes white again
for a few more hours.

Given the way things are

or might be, what could I do
on a dark road, a dark night
with the eyes of animals
staring at the headlights?
Or when I return, see the
state of the room,
papers and books on the floor,
socks loose without mates.
I might be tempted to look away or
seeing my work
scattered like those socks,
try for completion. I might
watch the fading light fade and
the rising sun rise.
It could be enough,
given the way things are,
to count the robins on the lawn,
wait for the toaster,
fry an omelet while
listening to a Schubert quartet, or
simply watch the day
become no more than
what it is, with or without
this mess, a day of strangers
passing on the sidewalk, aroma
of wood smoke on an October evening,
or perhaps just
the first mown lawn in spring.

The Unremembering

Could it be the end
that is really the beginning,
this unremembering, forgetting
which drawer holds the dessert forks
or where you parked the car?
And who was that beauty
who married Bogart?
The crowd on foot at The Globe
watching the Henry plays
had a name that's now just out of reach.
It doesn't matter. You were
waiting for the bus, talking easily
to the woman on the sidewalk.
Her hair was red and reminded you
of something you wanted
to tell her but the words
were missing so you just smiled.
There is life of a kind
in the blank left by such forgetting,
in what disappears, the town
your son moved to, the name
of the teacher who saved you
from the playground bullies,
the color of your first girlfriend's eyes.
They all go into the dark.
Then the bus arrives. You wave.
And climb aboard.

A Wrinkled Wing

Let January light
say what it has to say, but
not about sore knees or
vacant memory.
Let it speak, the winter sun,
soft as falling snow perhaps.
You do know
that light has a voice?
Sometimes quiet, as now,
or in summer when it
warms a wrinkled wing
that unfolds and
the Monarch discovers
her segmented body
is no longer worm,
leaf-bound and voracious,
but feather light
and lightly flying.

III: Encounters

Small Sounds

At night I am in a city
of small sounds—
one late bus carrying
three night-shift workers,
a door opening down the street,
guests laughing their goodbyes.
There is a highway
still humming as highways do,
but pianissimo. Our cars
tick-tick in the driveways
as engines cool.
One stops outside,
its radio still playing, muffled
behind closed windows.
A distant clang tells me
the racoons have begun their
nocturnal feeding.
The sounds of my night city
don't intrude.
There are no sirens
no drunken shouts
nothing like the roar
of a police helicopter
sitting over us,
its searchlight searching.
Nothing louder than the hiss
of the bus door opening,
a low rumble as it
heads for the next stop.

For a few months

perhaps a year,
I knew her name,
the girl in pink tights.
I remember the day she walked
splay-footed from the post office,
a lollipop in her mouth.
It was September,
a few weeks into school, a few
vestiges of summer hovering
the way vestiges do,
the heat of August,
cries from the soccer field, slow
conversation on the porches
at sunset. It must have been
lunchtime at school. She took a few
minutes to check the family mail or
perhaps just to get that lollipop
from the candy master
at the post office window.
I said hello, as I did now and then,
when we passed on the road, perhaps
made a bit of conversation. After all
they were new to our island town,
she and her family, and we
welcome newcomers.
I can still see her,
straggling toward me, her feet
pointing at nothing in particular,
face pointed at nothing
in particular. Now
they have left the island,
quietly, and I
have forgotten her name.

Frisbee

The boy sitting on the beach
wishing the others would
invite him over, that boy
could be wondering
how he is someone at all,
a boy in love with golden haired Barbara,
instead of a nobody,
being ignored.
But he is only a boy,
sitting alone with sand
getting into his trunks.
He hasn't yet encountered
Sisyphus and the absurd rock.
There is still hope for him,
if not Barbara then perhaps
a frisbee. It sails his way and
he snares it,
sails it perfectly back,
a flat, fast drill
with no wobbles
straight to the kid
surrounded by the cool girls
who catches it,
and throws it back,
grinning.

Planting Fireweed

You can learn about your own backyard by reading poems.
—Advice from a friend

You might be standing in that backyard,
reading poems to find the best
placement of a few shrubs and where
to plant your fireweed, which is also known
as rosebay willowherb, and takes you,
given the strange turns of mind,
to a Russian folktale.
It's Stravinsky's birthday,
which brings to mind *The Firebird,*
a tale that inspired him with
its balletic twists, fiery leaps, but
are you remembering that story or just
tracing the journey you took to get here,
your backyard, unsure of where to plant?
Stravinsky's not your favorite composer
you realize, as you look to place your
fireweed but one thing
leads to another, even to so simple
a discovery as that rosebay willowherb is not,
as you thought, loosestrife. And if
you continue down that road,
loose and strife-torn, you will learn
that what you hold now
was called bombweed,
in London during the blitz,
when it graced the ruins of bombed homes.
That disaster is now the gift
that waits in your backyard,
in your hands.
There is no need to read poems now.
It's time to get on your knees,
and plant.

The Case with Photographs

In the photo on the chest
(it doesn't matter what chest)
in the living room
(you needn't ask whose living room)
a man walks uphill in the snow
in a red coat, a blue cap.
There must be a camera somewhere, but
as is the case with photographs
you can't see it. Still, allow yourself
to picture that camera,
resting now on someone's hip.
Allow yourself to imagine that she
joins the man in the red coat.
There are trees in the frame but
you know by now that
the two have walked out of the picture
and perhaps out of the trees.
It's up to you, to your imagination
to bring them to their destination.
A narrow road, perhaps, where
a car is parked. A beach
the sea has cleared of snow.
It could be they are simply
walking to a small house
in a meadow, behind a stone wall.
Be generous with what you picture,
where you take them. Their lives
are in your hands.

Like a Sower

Summer's end picks up the pace
as it runs alongside fading light
while our northern trees
fold into orange and red.
I sit at an upstairs window,
watch an old woman
mowing the lawn next door.
When her son cuts
he's on the big John Deere,
enthroned above the grass.
He waves the steering wheel like a scepter
at each turn. She walks
peasant-like behind an ancient
gas job, back and forth
like a sower in an old painting,
scattering seed.
A student of age, I
read this lonely text,
try to see her face,
features, whether smiling or
fierce with pushing
but all I learn is
what a gray head looks like,
bent over a small
red machine.

Red Maserati

My father hums at the workbench,
spraying enamel from a paint can
onto a cylinder head.
The red Maserati sits behind him
quiet on the oil-spotted floor.
He wears no mask against the fumes
spewing from the can and he
doesn't think about the poison
he is breathing. He is lost
in his vision of an old car
brought to life.
The paint flows evenly
onto clean cast iron,
dries to a bright finish as the car
comes alive day by day,
as my father dies slowly,
humming at the workbench.

The Silver Pin

So she showed up in a dream,
the woman you talked to
in the produce section, but
no dream is just a dream. What if
you wake in the morning and
she's there, the produce woman,
standing on the sidewalk—are you
still dreaming? She looks so real,
no longer in blue jeans
and an Oriole's tee but
in a Laura Ashley dress,
with a little silver pin—is that a
swan? She asks if you're okay so
you know something was real
in that just-a-dream.
But that pin—swans mate for life,
drifting together before they
rise from the lake, wheeling in
great circles. Why do they leave,
you wonder, where are they going,
or are you dreaming again,
and is she really there,
smiling, on the sidewalk?

Holy Ground

Oh Jenny 's a' weet poor body
 Jenny 's seldom dry,
She draigl't a' her petticoatie
 Comin thro' the rye.
 —Robert Burns, "Comin Thro' the Rye"

It could have been holy ground,
the rye, when Jenny came through,
red hair flying, smile like the dawn.
Or is that wishful thinking,
appropriation of a folk song,
a fairy tale of heart's desires,
promises kept, dreams come true?
The sort of thing
a poet would make up.
And the rye? Holy ground
only until night closes in,
and the song is wet petticoats, Jenny
the beauty that will not come to him,
who lives in darkness.
"I thought you'd change," Beauty said,
"become worthy of me." But what poet
is ever that?
He's no more than a gray head,
trying to stay warm in a kitchen
where the fire is about to go out,
dreaming Jenny laughing and
running through the rye,
dragging her petticoats,
red hair flying.

The thing about tears

is we think we know what they mean
where they come from, but
they might just be the tears
from the cutting board where you
are peeling and slicing onions
for an onion pie for a friend
who's never heard of such a thing.
Or the roast vegetables for dinner
with your wife who was gone
for you can't remember how long
on the rocky beaches of Maine
looking for sea glass, or in
Southern California where surfers
slide into the green room.
But now she's here again,
and with tears of pleasure,
with or without
the onions.

IV: A Kind of Traverse

Standing Watch

Restless after dinner and because
the kitchen is too warm,
I walk to the clearing where three deer
are grazing. Two lower their heads
into clover, the third,
wide-eyed, ears erect,
stands watch.
He looks straight in my direction, but
I know he sees through me
to what lies beyond
this clearing.

A Congregation of Gulls

They don't know me, but
I watch while one
glides slowly down,
lands on the lake. She
just sits there the way
gulls do, floating with the
peace that wild things
have at times like these,
a cool November morning
between the noise of summer
and winter's hammer.
But she's not alone for long.
A second gull lands gracefully nearby,
and suddenly there are more,
in groups of two or three,
arriving at intervals,
like guests at a party.
And now a flotilla,
gulls sitting still or rising, one
after the other, wings flapping,
then resting again.
Two take off together,
fly around the party,
and return, having gone
perhaps into a corner,
seeing they had some private
business to discuss.
I'm not a guest, of course, although—
such being the world's intimacies—
we share a connection of sorts,
a sense of congregation.

The Hood

This January wind has its cold
hand on my neck.
I zip my jacket tighter,
put up the hood,
which helps, although it
seems to bother a crow
sitting in the trees.
He sets up the rapid cawing
that warns everyone. As for me,
I welcome the crow family,
their amiable chatter
as they go about crow business
on short hops from tree to tree.
They comment on the weather,
share the location of the kitchen scraps
or spread the word
about tonight's meeting to discuss
the seagull threat to the food supply.
One thing's for sure. They don't
seem bothered by this cold wind, so
what is it about a hood?
If that crow could see my face
he'd know I'm not dangerous,
could read my harmless intention
to find shelter and the nearest
cup of coffee. But of course
that's the problem. The hood
is all he sees and
for all I know
the last hood he saw
came with a gun.

Am I That Crow?

Tell me if I'm wrong, but did I
spend too much time looking out the window
when a crow's black shadow
caught my eye? Is it just
imagination, or am I now that crow
free to sail slowly down,

study with my curious dark eye
the open spaces in the grass?
I have nothing in mind except
to saunter across the road, rise easily
into a nearby tree. It takes
little effort to be a crow, just a

short hop into the branch I keep handy
for those occasions when a dog appears.
Save your breath, I tell myself,
for the family gathering this evening.
Save your energy to engage
the eagle who shows up

thinking to claim crow territory. I fly,
strut; I sit in trees and stare
knowing that what I see is
what there is to see. My crowness
is complete without fear or doubt,
nothing like what that man

behind the window might be fearing now,
as he watches me fly past.

More than Corn

The Crimson King Maple
knows (for all we know)
that we are here,
admiring its deep maroon leaves,
its wide embrace.
Or is it, perhaps, just content
to stand there drinking sunlight
while we make our human noises?
The wild geese have passed over
heading north, their cries echoing.
Do they need our fond attention?
The family dog asleep at someone's feet
dreams of the roaming pack,
ready to break free. We think
we know the mole's house,
the names of stars, but
check the moonlight around you,
odor of stubble in the field
come October. The grain in the silo
will be more than corn
even as it feeds your livestock.

And who's to say a storm

not just any, but the one
delivering an inch of rain
on a farm in Kansas—who
will say that storm doesn't
take direction from the weathercock
swinging on the barn ridge,
flashing when it turns
in the wind? All this chaos,
atmospheric disturbance,
hides in the predictable,
the pattern of streets,
spokes and grids laid out
for easy navigation by
emergency vehicles,
and in the recipe for pancakes,
the routine that brings me home
in time for the six o'clock news—
chaos hides in the ordinary pattern,
behind the squirrel that just
slipped from branch to branch
and did not fall as the wind subsided.
And while I'm not looking
the pattern could sneak by
in the shadow of my wife
as she opens a shoebox of old photos,
and laughs, remembering
trick-or-treaters at the door,
twenty Halloweens ago.
This murmuration, confusion of storms,
and of these odds and ends,
is like Facebook notifications
popping up on the screen—
starlings that somehow stick together
in one swirling cloud.

Beaufort Scale

*The Beaufort Scale of windspeed ranges
from Force 0 (Calm, smoke rises vertically)
to Force 12 (Hurricane, violent destruction)*

On a calm morning—
chimney smoke
straight as a young poplar,
the weather vane next door
motionless, its rooster quiet,
the lake still sleeping.
Some days the wind
is but a breath and I
walk quietly to hear
the leaves rustle, watch
the lake form glassy wavelets,
the trees, how the small
twigs move, the schoolhouse flag
stretch itself. Small
branches sway, dust and loose
paper scatter at my feet,
while the lake gallops
like white horses.
At the ocean, waves
take a long form,
release puffs of spray,
grow larger, grow white crests.
The sea heaps up, the wind
pushes, walking
is difficult. Foam streaks
waves' faces and the sea rolls.
I think of shingles
blown off roofs,
trees uprooted.
Waves crest, hang snarling,

hide the small ship
that struggles to windward.
It's time to seek shelter and
I do, praying for protection
of a world now invisible
behind foam and spray.

When This Day Is Over

After this storm, these clouds
heavy with the fate
of a small island—
the downed power lines,
refrigerators thawing
while the houses grow cold
and the postmaster keeps watch
in a room without mail,
while spruce branches break
under the weight of snow
and the hum of generators
muffles the low roar of surf—
we will shovel out and
toss the meat gone bad,
put the coffee on and
visit in quiet kitchens.
When this day is over.

The Shape of Silence

I expect it to show up
as I lie in the dark, in
a kind of traverse
across unmarked snow.
I could be on a knife ridge
high above a frozen river,
sure-footed, the stillness
taking shape in the cold.
There is a gathering
of sorts, unheard whispers,
the furnace exhaling as it
shuts off, a leaf falling,
sounds forming the silence
the way silence forms, as in
the requiem when Mozart died,
eight bars into the Lacrimosa, silence now
become a shape on the breath,
between heart beats. Or in Salzburg
when Marian Anderson stopped singing,
leaving the crucifixion hanging in silence,
the listeners, in awe, hands still,
facing the wordless shape of Calvary,
without a sound.
I open a book and
look in the words for a
silence so large and
shapely I can walk into it
as into a forest,
to a lake whose waters
fill what remains.

In a Kitchen

For Ann Fernald

You say you're looking for intimacy?
It won't show up right away.
Give it time, give it
space, but not at the mall with its
turbulent, endless corridors.
Can you see from one end to the other
through those windows full of
shoes and dresses, toys and games,
through all the people?
You can walk for hours,
looking for who knows what.
You might as well hope for intimacy
in North Dakota on the prairie,
and what about the sea?
It might be calm tonight
but it won't be intimate, won't be
just any space, your living room or
cruising in your Chevy
with your date—no.
Wait until you're at the end of things,
then turn back down the road,
the one that leads through the heart of town,
past the post office, school,
the small library. Take with you
that sense of being closed in.
After a while, when you've
stopped looking for the nearest
Starbucks, slice of pizza, someone
will invite you into her kitchen,
give you a cup of coffee,
tell you what the neighbors are up to,
while the biscuits bake and
robins gather on the lawn.

Sunrise, Damariscotta

The lake this morning
sleeps without a ripple
in its bed of earth and eelgrass.
Loons will row out later from
tiny islands of woven twigs and
sweet rush to wake the surface,
and a breeze will follow.
But now nothing stirs except
what lies below,
like the memories
deep in an old man's mind.

A Robin Stalks the Lawn

He listens for his dinner, and reminds me
that nourishment, in whatever form,
fleshy worm or cloudy thought,
is present to the attentive ear.
The sound might begin
somewhere through the grass,
in the earth below or
in the clouds themselves.
If there is an art to hearing
one's next meal or some
food for the imagination,
the trick
(something tells me)
is to stalk quietly,
or perhaps just sit,
as I do now,
in a room of blue walls,
curtains that sway in a warm breeze
and propose a quiet mind.
There is a voice, they suggest
and in time it will speak.

V: Somehow Balanced

"Take me back"

she said, but I
thought she meant back home.
I pulled off at the nearest
wide shoulder, turned around
and we drove back,
across the bridge
and through the blueberry barrens
past yards where boats sat on their trailers
like beached whales
getting cold and sullen
under blue tarps,
past the abandoned chicken barn,
the sorry ranch houses with their gray
satellite dishes. We climbed the ridge
and saw the bay stretched out like
a blue tablecloth but
"No," she said, "Not here.
I meant back. Don't you know?
Back is not a place, is it?
I'm not ready to go home.
Let's keep driving for a while.
I know we'll find it if we
just keep going."

On the Sheepscot Road

In my long history
of mistakes, this one
came early, as a teenage
rite of passage into
fumbling adulthood. It was
the botched replacement
of the distributor in my
first car. I was proud
of myself. The car
started right up and
I set off confident, but
somewhere on the Sheepscot Road
a fierce knocking began,
followed by denial—"It's just
something needing adjustment."
Would the outcome have been
different if I'd just pulled off and
stopped before a connecting rod came loose
and punched through the engine block?
Would my life have been
a history not of broken engines
but of polished chrome, children
laughing on playground swings,
perfectly formed bread loaves
fresh from the oven? If
I'd just learned to heed
the warning signs, tightened
my belt and taken care of things
before they broke?
Now the old Chevy sits in the woods
motionless when I visit,
marking my threescore and ten.

It looks strangely content in rust
and blistered paint. It slowly
fades among the trees, it sinks
into the forgiving earth.

A Bounded Space

For the island people of Islesford, Maine

It starts at the end,
at the beach, say, or
the island dock
where the unknown begins
and we turn back.
We've reached a boundary of sorts,
could break loose in the inflatable,
slide out of harbor on a jet ski—
but we know we'd just be
ignoring the border,
between loneliness and intimacy.
We're students of attachment,
as between atomic particles
or the companionship of stars.
"We can't go out today,"
we say at breakfast, meaning
the seas are too big,
the border is closed.
We're in a bounded space,
not trapped although
we rarely go abroad.

Drink Me

There was a small wagon
full of petunias and nasturtiums,
Sweet William. We had pulled off
to buy tomatoes at a farm stand.
It was raining, but the flowers
didn't mind.
They were almost laughing
the way children laugh
running through the rain,
mouths open to catch the drops.
The glaze on delicate petals
brought out the colors,
yellow and blue,
rose, bright as
faces on the playground.
I felt transformed, or
would have been if
like Alice I'd had a bottle
of "Drink Me."
I wouldn't hesitate, but
gladly take a sip and,
now the right size,
crawl into that wagon
to lie in summer rain
with the flowers.

Ex Libris

She asks whether I have
a stack of books, but
the lamp on the small table
has a habit of resisting stacks.
They pile in corners instead, like
fresh snow—the stories, drifts of poetry,
essays. They meditate, exchange wisdom and
nonsense up and down
among themselves while
flies and dust join in as they can.
Or they scatter, the books,
some in the bathroom,
the coffee table, on the counter,
waiting for the English muffin to brown.
Their *modus operandi* is stillness,
the comfort of a dignified
built-in mahogany bookcase or
in that clutter of magazines
on the floor.
Books, after all, are knowledgeable,
and what they know are people,
how unpredictable we are,
unsteady with words,
changing the dialogue, the plot,
grabbing a book on the way to
the doctor's or dropping one absently
when the doorbell rings,
while they wait patiently
for our return,
and the start of the next chapter.

At Bradley's Used Books

in the old church with its
empty belfry where the rooks
lead their clamorous lives,
a dictionary sits.
It never moves although
I look every time I visit Bradley's.
Perhaps the clientele
know how quickly words change, and
are wary of an old dictionary, even one
as distinguished as this, in its deep blue
cloth boards, gold lettering, one word,
"Oxford," sitting with great assurance
at the base of the spine.
Sometimes I stop to
keep company with the book,
take comfort in its presence,
whether permanent or temporary,
while the rooks
busy themselves above me,
sometimes chattering
in rook language,
sometimes as silent
as this old dictionary.

Searching for Radiance

I was, and
always had been,
searching for radiance,
though the looking could be falling
when I swiveled too quickly as
a leaping deer caught my eye.
Balance is my short suit,
staring too hard
as a tree turns from green
to gold to leafless, although
wandering the unbalanced road
does finally lead me
somewhere—though where is not
always given me to say.
By any route, direct or
dark, with a foot down,
another following, finding
the right place, right time,
I come to know
when it's my turn and
everything around me
is radiant.

Four and Twenty Black Birds

They flock onto the grass like
kids around the ice cream truck,
first one, then a trio, then,
suddenly,
two dozen or more.
And who's to say that four and twenty
black birds are not kids at heart,
expecting something toothsome
outside my window?
They are, indeed,
black,
but what black signifies
cannot take much space
in a crow's mind.
I know they know
I'm here and will—
if I go for a closer look—
be gone as one,
tuned as one mind
to all dangers, no matter how slight.
Things black to me,
the signs of fears I cloak in black,
beaked and croaking murder,
are no more to a crow
than neighbors, kinfolk, and the
chance to gather
for a few sweet morsels
on some guy's lawn.

Flying

It matters nothing to him,
that the flock of terns he chases
will just fly away.
There are his own flying legs,
perfectly formed flanks—
though a dog doesn't think
about such things.
That's all in my head.
What matters, the running,
the instinct to seize,
belongs to him although we
share, he and I
the thing we call pleasure,
now his in his doggy knowing,
mine in my watching
as he flies down the beach,
with the blue Atlantic,
roaring beside him.

Somehow Balanced

A hawk hangs motionless
between cloud and roadway,
as I watch motionless
from a roadside table.

What holds us up,
the weightless and the weighty,
the hawk all eye and wing,
and me, the brooding sitter?

We float together, one
in endless sky, one
in the clear sky of the mind,
each in a different flying,

held up somehow as one,
and somehow balanced.

Envoy

Driven Rain

Somewhere on the road
In rain driven against me
Was a solitude
A shelter in the howling.

And a voice could be heard
In that darkness
Faint but
Very like singing.

The song was
Fully present then
Fully wind and
Driven rain.

About the Author

Now retired from a career teaching college English, Ralph Stevens lives in Ellsworth, Maine with his wife, the photographer Sally Rowan. Stevens has been nominated for a Pushcart Prize and is the author of the collections *At Bunker Cove* (Moon Pie Press, 2017), *Things Haven't Been the Same* (Finishing Line Press, 2020), and *Water under Snow* (Wipf and Stock: Resource Publications, 2021). He is a regular contributor to the online journal *Verse Virtual,* and his poems have appeared in a variety of publications and on the radio programs *The Writer's Almanac* and *Poems from Here.* Ralph's poetry reflects and is inspired by the natural world and by an interest in the role of consciousness in the relationship between the human and non-human. For him the "non-human" is not just the wildlife—the loons, deer, crows that appear in his poems—but even that world we think of as "unconscious": trees, corn, the wind itself.

Ralph can be reached at:
thismansart@gmail.com
(207) 479-5843
www.facebook.com/ralph.stevens.146

www.ingramcontent.com/pod-product-compliance
Lightning Source LLC
Chambersburg PA
CBHW030911170426
43193CB00009BA/809